Success With

Math

SCHOLASTIC

Editor: Ourania Papacharalambous
Cover design by Tannaz Fassihi; cover illustration by Kevin Zimmer
Interior design by Cynthia Ng
Interior illustrations by Mette Engell (5, 36–37); Doug Jones (8, 24, 26, 31, 34); Gabriele Tafuni (13)
All other images @ Shutterstock.com

ISBN 978-1-338-79852-4
Scholastic Inc., 557 Broadway, New York, NY 10012
Copyright © 2022 Scholastic Inc.
All rights reserved. Printed in the U.S.A.
First printing, January 2022
2 3 4 5 6 7 8 9 10   40   29 28 27 26 25 24 23

INTRODUCTION

Parents and teachers alike will find *Scholastic Success With Math* to be a valuable educational tool. It is designed to help students in the fourth grade improve their math skills. The practice pages incorporate challenging puzzles, inviting games, riddles, and more that students are sure to enjoy. On page 4, you will find a list of the key skills covered in the activities throughout this book. Students will practice skills such as place value, multiplication, division, fractions, and decimals. They are also challenged to use bar graphs, identify patterns, find perimeter and area, and much more! Remember to praise students for their efforts and successes!

TABLE OF CONTENTS

Grade-Appropriate Skills Covered in
Scholastic Success With Math: Grade 4

Fluently add and subtract multi-digit whole numbers using the standard algorithm.

Solve multi-step word problems posed with whole numbers and having whole-number answers using the four operations.

Recognize that a whole number is a multiple of each of its factors.

Determine whether a given whole number in the range 1—100 is a multiple of a given one-digit number.

Recognize that in a multi-digit whole number, a digit in one place represents ten times what it represents in the place to its right.

Use place value understanding to round multi-digit whole numbers to any place.

Compare two multi-digit numbers based on meanings of the digits in each place.

Compare two fractions with different numerators and different denominators. Recognize that comparisons are valid only when the two fractions refer to the same whole.

Understand addition and subtraction of fractions as joining and separating parts referring to the same whole.

Decompose a fraction into a sum of fractions with the same denominator.

Solve word problems involving addition and subtraction of fractions referring to the same whole and having like denominators.

Know relative sizes of measurement units within one system of units including km, m, cm; kg, g; lb, oz.; l, ml; hr, min, sec. Within a single system of measurement, express measurements in a larger unit in terms of a smaller unit.

Use the four operations to solve word problems involving distances, intervals of time, liquid volumes, masses of objects, and money, including problems involving simple fractions or decimals, and problems that require expressing measurements given in a larger unit in terms of a smaller unit.

Solve problems involving addition and subtraction of fractions by using information presented in line plots or bar graphs.

Recognize angles as geometric shapes that are formed wherever two rays share a common endpoint.

Understand that an angle is measured with reference to a circle with its center at the common endpoint of the rays by considering the fraction of the circular arc between the points where the two rays intersect the circle. Understand that an angle that turns through n one-degree angles is said to have an angle measure of n degrees.

Measure angles in whole-number degrees using a protractor.

Classify two-dimensional figures based on the presence or absence of parallel or perpendicular lines, or the presence or absence of angles of a specified size. Recognize right triangles as a category, and identify right triangles.

Recognize a line of symmetry for a two-dimensional figure as a line across the figure such that the figure can be folded along the line into matching parts. Identify line-symmetric figures and draw lines of symmetry.

Mystery Numbers

Use the digits in the list below to answer each number riddle.
Digits appear only once in an answer. Each answer may not use all digits.

$$2 \quad 4 \quad 9 \quad 6 \quad 7 \quad 3$$

1 When you subtract a 2-digit number from a 3-digit number, the difference is 473.

What are the numbers? _____

2 The sum of these two numbers is 112.

What are the numbers? _____

3 The sum of these two numbers is 519.

What are the numbers? _____

4 The difference between these two 3-digit numbers is 263.

What are the numbers? _____

5 The sum of these three 2-digit numbers is 184.

What are the numbers? _____

6 The difference between two 3-digit numbers is a palindrome between 200 and 300.

What are the numbers? _____

A Place for Every Number

Look at the numbers in 243. Each number in the group has its own "place" and meaning. For instance, the 2 in 243 is in the hundreds place. That stands for 2 hundreds, or 200. The 4 is in the tens place, meaning 4 tens, or 40. And the 3 is in the ones place, meaning 3 ones, or 3.

Use a place value chart to put the numbers in this cross-number puzzle in their places.

ACROSS

A. 3 hundreds 2 tens 6 ones

C. 8 tens 1 one

E. 6 tens 4 ones

F. 4 tens 7 ones

H. 5 hundreds 2 tens 6 ones

J. 9 tens 3 ones

K. 8 tens 9 ones

M. 5 hundreds 4 tens 2 ones

O. 2 thousands 8 hundreds
   3 tens 1 one

Q. 9 tens 8 ones

S. 6 hundreds 6 tens 4 ones

DOWN

A. 3 tens 6 ones

B. 2 thousands 4 hundreds
   5 tens 7 ones

D. 1 hundred 4 tens 9 ones

G. 7 tens 3 ones

I. 6 thousands 8 hundreds
   5 tens 1 one

L. 9 tens 4 ones

N. 2 hundreds 9 tens 6 ones

P. 3 tens 5 ones

R. 8 tens 4 ones

Bee Riddle

Round each number.
To solve the riddle, find the question number at the bottom of the page. Then, use your answers and the Decoder to fill in the blanks.

1. Round 7 to the nearest ten _____

2. Round 23 to the nearest ten _____

3. Round 46 to the nearest ten _____

4. Round 92 to the nearest ten _____

5. Round 203 to the nearest hundred _____

6. Round 420 to the nearest hundred _____

7. Round 588 to the nearest hundred _____

8. Round 312 to the nearest hundred _____

9. Round 549 to the nearest hundred _____

10. Round 710 to the nearest hundred _____

Decoder

400	A
800	W
30	O
10	Y
25	E
500	I
210	J
20	L
40	C
700	U
90	S
100	T
600	G
95	F
50	N
550	V
300	Z
7	H
200	Z

What did the farmer get when he tried to reach the beehive?

A "B___ ___ ___ ___"   ___ ___ ___ ___ ___ ___
    10 5 8 1   4 9 7 3 6 2

Number Patterns

Write the next number on the line. Then, circle the plus or minus sign and write what you added or subtracted to get it. The first one is done for you.

1 1, 9, 17, 25, 33, __41__ ⊕– __8__

2 75, 80, 85, 90, 95, _____ + – _____

3 47, 53, 59, 65, 71, _____ + – _____

4 70, 73, 76, 79, 82, _____ + – _____

5 93, 88, 83, 78, 73, _____ + – _____

6 98, 92, 86, 80, 74, _____ + – _____

7 29, 38, 47, 56, 65, _____ + – _____

8 30, 38, 46, 54, 62, _____ + – _____

9 75, 71, 67, 63, 59, _____ + – _____

10 51, 58, 65, 72, 79, _____ + – _____

11 11, 20, 29, 38, 47, _____ + – _____

12 57, 55, 53, 51, 49, _____ + – _____

13 35, 39, 43, 47, 51, _____ + – _____

14 87, 79, 71, 63, 55, _____ + – _____

15 99, 90, 81, 72, 63, _____ + – _____

16 73, 75, 77, 79, 81, _____ + – _____

17 68, 61, 54, 47, 40, _____ + – _____

18 32, 41, 50, 59, 68, _____ + – _____

19 65, 62, 59, 56, 53, _____ + – _____

20 42, 47, 52, 57, 62, _____ + – _____

Root for the Home Team!

Use the coordinates to identify points on the graph. The first number is along the horizontal axis.

To solve the riddle, find the question number at the bottom of the page. Then, use the letter at each point on the graph to fill in the blanks.

1 (1, 1) _____

2 (3, 4) _____

3 (4, 7) _____

4 (6, 2) _____

5 (5, 5) _____

6 (2, 5) _____

7 (0, 3) _____

8 (1, 7) _____

9 (7, 6) _____

10 (5, 0) _____

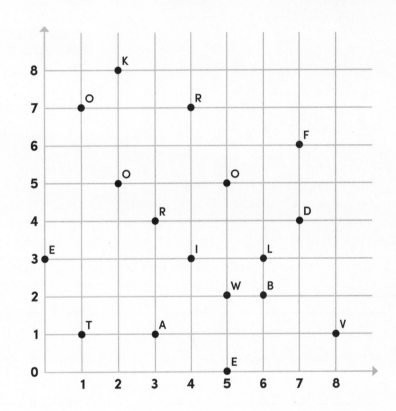

What do cheerleaders like to drink?

Lots ___ ___   ___ ___ ___ ___   ___ ___ ___ ___
    5 9   2 6 8 1   4 7 10 3

Food to Go

Figure it out!

1. Woovis the Dog found a $5 bill. Which item can he buy from the menu that will give the least change?

_____

DOGGIE DINER MENU

Kibble...................$1.79
Mouse Crumbs........$1.39
Table Scraps..........$2.49
Crumbs & Cheese...$3.19
Deluxe Scraps........$3.79

2. Molly Mouse gets Crumbs and Cheese for breakfast. She pays with the $5 bill. With the leftover money, what can Woovis buy to eat?

_____

3. Which item can Woovis buy with the $5 bill that will give the most change?

_____

4. Which two items can Woovis buy with the $5 bill so that he gets about $1 back in change?

_____

5. Woovis ordered two items from the menu and gave the cashier the $5 bill. But the two items cost more than $6.50. Which two items did Woovis order?

_____

Bathtub Brunch

Find each sum.
To solve the riddle, find the question number at the bottom of the page. Then, use your answers and the Decoder to fill in the blanks.

Decoder

5,429	A	689	N
10,493	F	2,009	B
2,133	S	8,292	O
14,983	R	3,234	I
10,439	P	7,538	G
712	U	1,804	C
3,489	K	4,708	H
1,840	M	6,521	L
1,063	E	8,234	E
4,523	W		

1. 1,004 + 800 = _____

2. 512 + 177 = _____

3. 364 + 699 = _____

4. 1,245 + 888 = _____

5. 1,876 + 1,613 = _____

6. 2,010 + 6,224 = _____

7. 5,470 + 2,068 = _____

8. 4,526 + 3,766 = _____

9. 1,017 + 4,412 = _____

10. 2,588 + 7,851 = _____

What's the best thing to eat in a bathtub?

___ ___ ___ ___ ___ ___   ___ ___ ___ ___
4   10   8   2   7   6   1   9   5   3

What a Diamond!

Subtract. Color the picture. Use the color key.

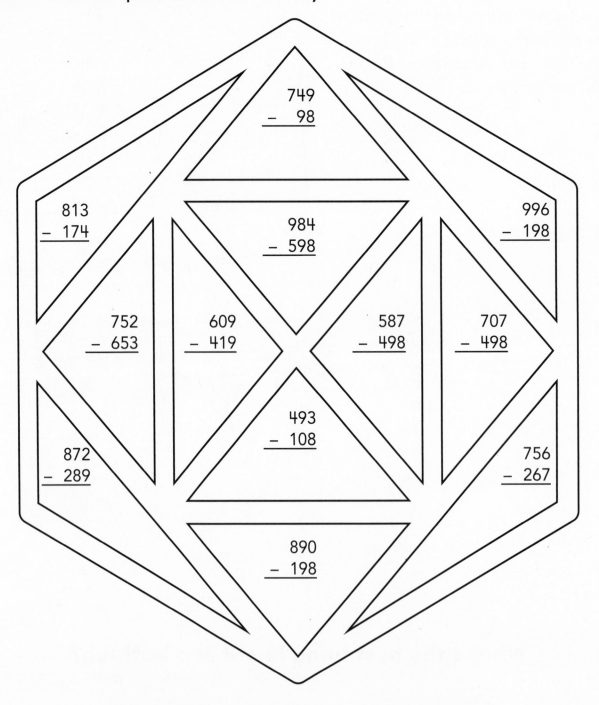

If the difference is between	Color the space
1 and 400	red
401 and 800	black

Cross-Number Puzzle

Subtract. Complete the puzzle.

ACROSS

2. 3,016
  − 1,209

6. 246,342
  − 156,129

8. 64,293
  − 28,318

9. 5,249
  − 3,928

10. 36,425
  − 18,929

11. 5,264
  − 3,192

12. 818,462
  − 131,910

14. 3,642
  − 1,813

15. 7,645
  − 1,328

DOWN

1. 6,429
  − 3,298

3. 9,145
  − 2,189

4. 9,142
  − 1,381

5. 58,142
  − 13,098

7. 76,418
  − 39,291

10. 31,642
  − 18,945

13. 814,603
  − 148,231

My Garden Plan

Multiply. Color the picture. Use the color key.

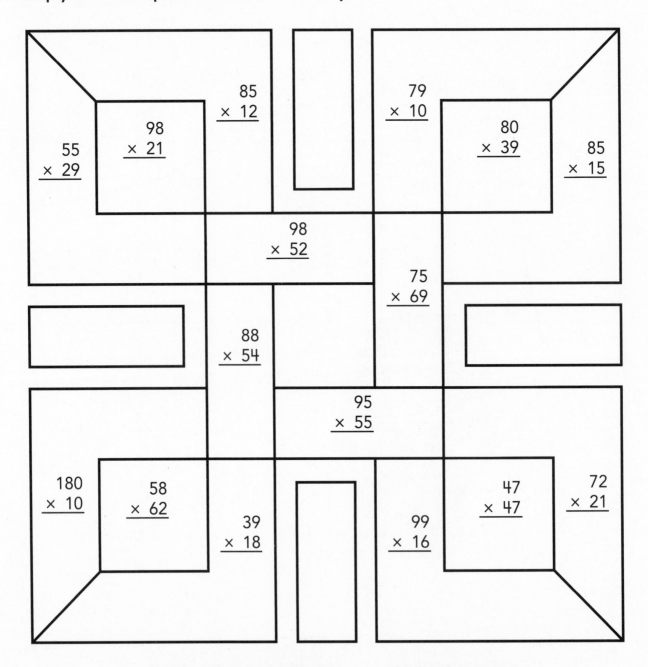

85
× 12

79
× 10

98
× 21

80
× 39

55
× 29

85
× 15

98
× 52

75
× 69

88
× 54

95
× 55

180
× 10

58
× 62

47
× 47

72
× 21

39
× 18

99
× 16

If the answer is between	Color the space
1 and 2000	purple
2001 and 4000	yellow
4001 and 6000	blue

Fill in the other spaces with colors of your choice.

Octagon Multiplication

Multiply. Color the picture. Use the color key.

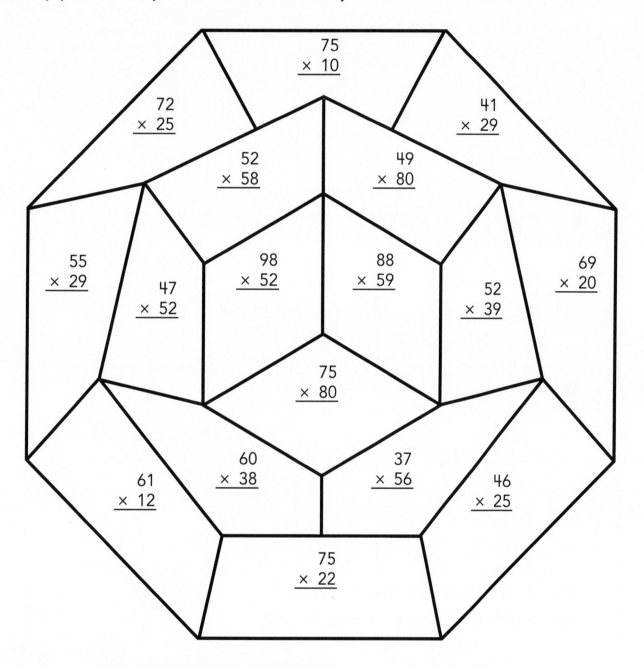

If the answer is between	Color the space
1 and 2000	purple
2001 and 4000	orange
4001 and 6000	red

Fill in the other spaces with colors of your choice.

A Dairy Life

Find the missing factor or dividend. Then, use the code to solve the riddle below.

D _____ × 2 = 22	**E** $4\overline{)5}$
G _____ × 7 = 84	**A** $2\overline{)2}$
H _____ × 4 = 36	**N** $3\overline{)6}$
I _____ × 3 = 24	**O** _____ ÷ 1 = 7
M _____ × 2 = 10	**Y** _____ ÷ 4 = 12
R _____ × 3 = 18	**T** _____ ÷ 1 = 3

What gives milk, says "moo," and makes wishes come true?

___ ___ ___ ___ ___ ___
 4   11 4   8   6   48

___ ___ ___ ___ ___ ___ ___ ___ ___
12   7   11 5   7   3   9   20 6

Division Decoder

Find each quotient.
To solve the riddle, find the question number at the bottom of the page. Then, use your answers and the Decoder to fill in the blanks.

1 $8 \div 2 =$ _____

2 $10 \div 5 =$ _____

3 $24 \div 4 =$ _____

4 $50 \div 10 =$ _____

5 $72 \div 9 =$ _____

6 $32 \div 8 =$ _____

7 $48 \div 7 =$ _____

8 $29 \div 3 =$ _____

9 $65 \div 8 =$ _____

10 $92 \div 6 =$ _____

Decoder

8 I	1 .... F
3 remainder 2 L	7 remainder 6 ..... N
7 .... W	6 remainder 6 I
8 remainder 1 ..... S	2 .... E
6 .... U	11 .... O
9 .... A	15 remainder 2 ... P
15 remainder 3 ... B	2 remainder 5 X
4 L	10 C
2 remainder 3 .... D	5 .... R
9 remainder 2 ..... T	

What kind of tools do you use for math?

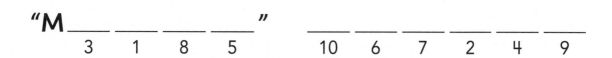

"M ___ ___ ___ ___ "   ___ ___ ___ ___ ___ ___
   3   1   8   5   10   6   7   2   4   9

Flower Division

**Divide. Color the picture.
Use the color key.**

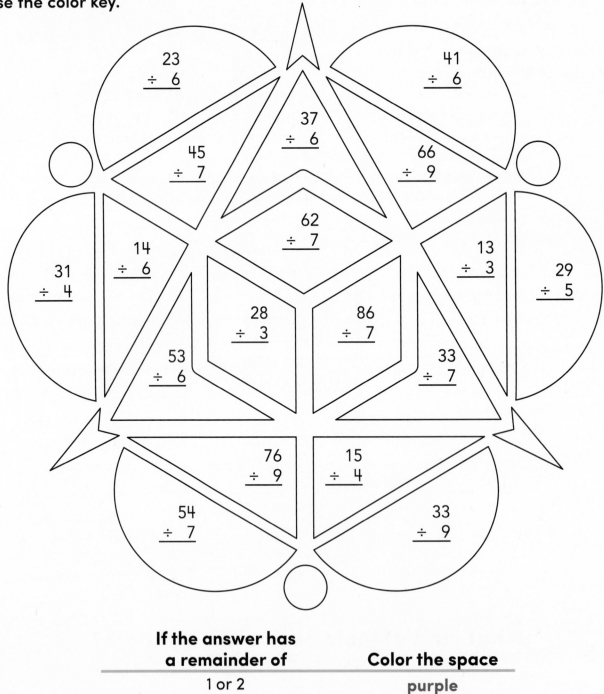

If the answer has a remainder of	Color the space
1 or 2	purple
3 or 4	blue
5 or 6	yellow

Fill in the other spaces with colors of your choice.

A Parade of Crabs

Read the passage. Then, write an equation and the answer for each word problem below.

Look for clue words to help you decide which operation to use. For example:

There are 15 crabs on one road and 6 crabs on another road. Each crab has 8 legs.

- How many crabs are there in total? **Total** signals addition: 15 + 6 = 21 crabs
- How many more are there on the first road? **How many more** tells us to find the difference, or subtract: 15 – 6 = 9 crabs
- How many legs do 9 crabs have in all? **In all** signals multiplication: 8 × 9 = 72 legs
- A crab's body has 2 sides. There are an equal number of legs on each side. How many legs are there per side? **Per** signals division: 8 ÷ 2 = 4 legs

Every year, millions of red crabs go on the march on Christmas Island, a part of Australia. In late October or early November, the cherry-red crabs migrate almost three miles from the forest in the center of the island to the beach. Their mission: to breed and lay eggs in the waters of the Indian Ocean.

The crabs crawl over or through everything in their paths—schools, homes, and even busy roads. People on the island are careful not to step on or drive over the crabs during this time.

After hatching in the ocean, millions of baby crabs the size of fingernails emerge from the water. They follow the same route their parents took as they head into the forest. There they grow into adults and start the cycle again.

1 When a baby red crab leaves the ocean, it is 4 millimeters long. About 3 days later, its length is 4 millimeters greater. How long is it then? _____

2 A female red crab can lay up to 100,000 eggs in one season! She might lay eggs about 8 times in her life. How many eggs can she lay in all her life? _____

3 Coconut crabs also live on Christmas Island. They use their pincers to open coconuts. An adult coconut crab is 40 inches long. That's 8 times the length of an adult red crab. How long is an adult red crab? _____

Food Fractions

ACTIVITY GOAL
Identify the fraction represented in each shape
to complete a riddle.

> The **denominator** of each
> fraction represents the
> total amount of parts in the
> shape. The shaded parts
> represent the **numerator**.
> A food item can help
> illustrate the strategy.

EXAMPLE
There are 8 slices of pie shown here; ($\frac{}{8}$) is the
denominator. The shaded area represents how many
pieces of the pie you can eat; ($\frac{1}{}$) is the numerator.
The fraction represented in this picture is $\frac{1}{8}$.

TRY THIS!
Draw a pizza on another sheet of paper, then cut out the circle. Cut the pizza into six equal
pieces. Using your paper pizza, make the following fractions: $\frac{1}{2}$, $\frac{2}{3}$, $\frac{5}{6}$, $\frac{1}{3}$.
Now divide your pizza between you and two imaginary friends.

Did you each get the same amount? _____

MORE SWEET FUN!
Color $\frac{1}{3}$ of these 12 pieces of candy. What fraction of the candy is left? _____

Now that you've reviewed fractions, duck in to action and name a few fractions to solve
the riddle on the following page!

Duck Into Action With Fractions

Why don't ducks like to get mail? Fractions can help you find the answer. Each of the shapes below represent a fraction and a letter. To figure out each fraction, compare the number of shaded spaces in the shape to the total number of spaces.

Example: is the same as $\frac{2}{6}$. Next write the letter that is underneath each shape on the corresponding blank below. You will use some letters several times. Now get quacking!

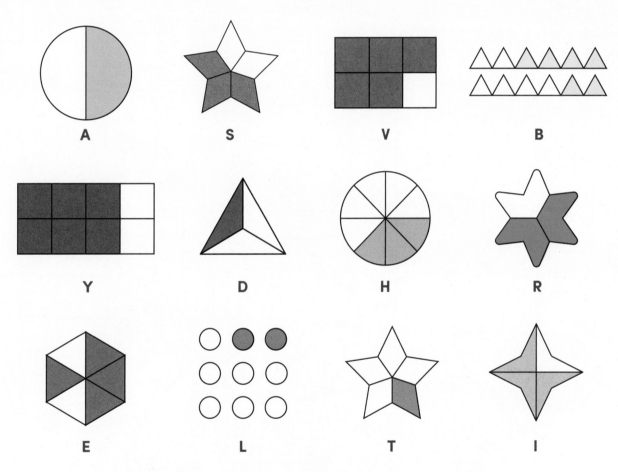

Why don't ducks like to get mail?

$$\frac{1}{5} \quad \frac{3}{8} \quad \frac{4}{6} \quad \frac{6}{8} \qquad \frac{1}{2} \quad \frac{2}{9} \quad \frac{2}{3} \quad \frac{4}{6} \quad \frac{1}{2} \quad \frac{1}{3} \quad \frac{6}{8}$$

$$\frac{3}{8} \quad \frac{1}{2} \quad \frac{5}{6} \quad \frac{4}{6} \qquad \frac{6}{12} \quad \frac{3}{4} \quad \frac{2}{9} \quad \frac{2}{9} \quad \frac{3}{5} \cdot$$

Hanging Quilt

Color the picture. Use the color key.

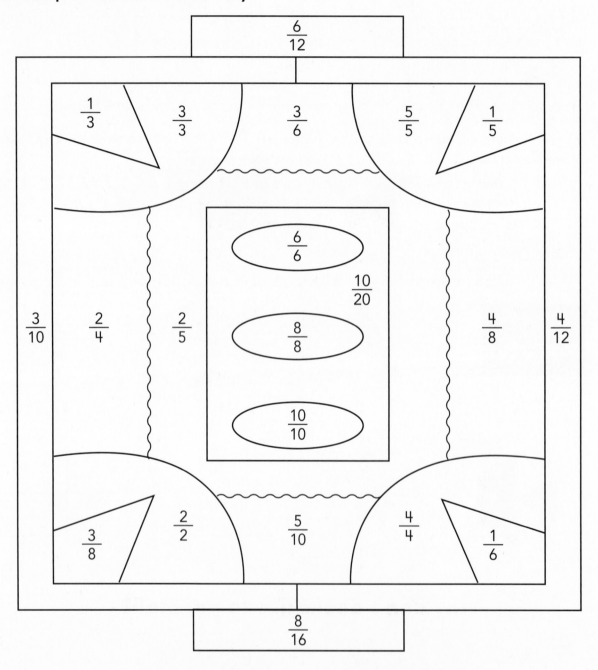

If the answer is	Color the space
$= \frac{1}{2}$	blue
$= 1$	red
$< \frac{1}{2}$	yellow

Add It Up!

When adding fractions with the same denominator, add the numerators. The denominator does not change. If necessary, reduce to lowest terms.

$$\frac{1}{6} + \frac{2}{6} = \frac{3}{6} \qquad\qquad \frac{3}{6} = \frac{1}{2}$$

When the numerator and the denominator are the same number, the fraction has a value of 1. When the numerator is equal to, or greater than the denominator, the fraction is called an **improper fraction**. When a number has two parts, a whole number and a fraction, it is called a **mixed number**.

$\frac{9}{7}$ can be changed to a mixed number by dividing the numerator by the denominator.

$$7\overline{)\begin{array}{r} 1 \\ 9 \\ -7 \\ \hline 2 \end{array}} = 1\frac{2}{7}$$

Add. Change each improper fraction to a mixed number. Reduce to lowest terms.

1 $\quad \frac{2}{5} + \frac{2}{5} = \underline{\qquad}$

2 $\quad \frac{1}{8} + \frac{7}{8} = \underline{\qquad}$

3 $\quad \frac{3}{4} + \frac{2}{4} = \underline{\qquad}$

4 $\quad \frac{3}{7} + \frac{2}{7} = \underline{\qquad}$

5 $\quad \frac{2}{5} + \frac{4}{5} = \underline{\qquad}$

6 $\quad \frac{8}{9} + \frac{10}{9} = \underline{\qquad}$

7 $\quad \frac{3}{6} + \frac{2}{6} = \underline{\qquad}$

8 $\quad \frac{4}{7} + \frac{6}{7} = \underline{\qquad}$

9 $\quad \frac{5}{6} + \frac{4}{6} = \underline{\qquad}$

10 $\quad \frac{5}{12} + \frac{3}{12} = \underline{\qquad}$

11 $\quad \frac{8}{10} + \frac{6}{10} = \underline{\qquad}$

12 $\quad \frac{3}{9} + \frac{1}{9} = \underline{\qquad}$

13 $\quad \frac{8}{11} + \frac{5}{11} = \underline{\qquad}$

14 $\quad \frac{3}{10} + \frac{2}{10} = \underline{\qquad}$

15 $\quad \frac{4}{8} + \frac{6}{8} = \underline{\qquad}$

You Can Do It!

To add fractions when the denominators are different, find equivalent fractions with common denominators. Then, add and reduce to lowest terms, if necessary.

$$\frac{1}{2}$$
$$+ \frac{1}{4}$$

$$\frac{1 \times 2}{2 \times 2} = \frac{2}{4}$$
$$+ \frac{1}{4} \qquad + \frac{1}{4}$$

$$\frac{2}{4}$$
$$+ \frac{1}{4}$$
$$\frac{3}{4}$$

Find equivalent fractions with common denominators. Add. Reduce to lowest terms, then use the code to solve the riddle.

L $\frac{1}{4}$ $+ \frac{1}{8}$ $+$ ___

D $\frac{1}{3}$ $+ \frac{1}{9}$ $+$ ___

S $\frac{1}{5}$ $+ \frac{1}{10}$ $+$ ___

I $\frac{1}{8}$ $+ \frac{1}{16}$ $+$ ___

C $\frac{1}{4}$ $+ \frac{1}{12}$ $+$ ___

R $\frac{1}{2}$ $+ \frac{1}{8}$ $+$ ___

E $\frac{1}{5}$ $+ \frac{1}{15}$ $+$ ___

T $\frac{1}{2}$ $+ \frac{1}{10}$ $+$ ___

E $\frac{1}{3}$ $+ \frac{1}{6}$ $+$ ___

I $\frac{1}{4}$ $+ \frac{1}{16}$ $+$ ___

N $\frac{1}{3}$ $+ \frac{1}{12}$ $+$ ___

N $\frac{1}{2}$ $+ \frac{1}{12}$ $+$ ___

What is so fragile that you break it when you say its name?

___ ___ ___ ___ ___ ___ ___
$\frac{3}{10}$ $\frac{3}{16}$ $\frac{3}{8}$ $\frac{1}{2}$ $\frac{7}{12}$ $\frac{1}{3}$ $\frac{4}{15}$

Out of This World

Subtract and reduce to lowest terms.
Use the chart to color the picture.

To subtract fractions with like denominators, subtract the numerators. The denominator does not change.

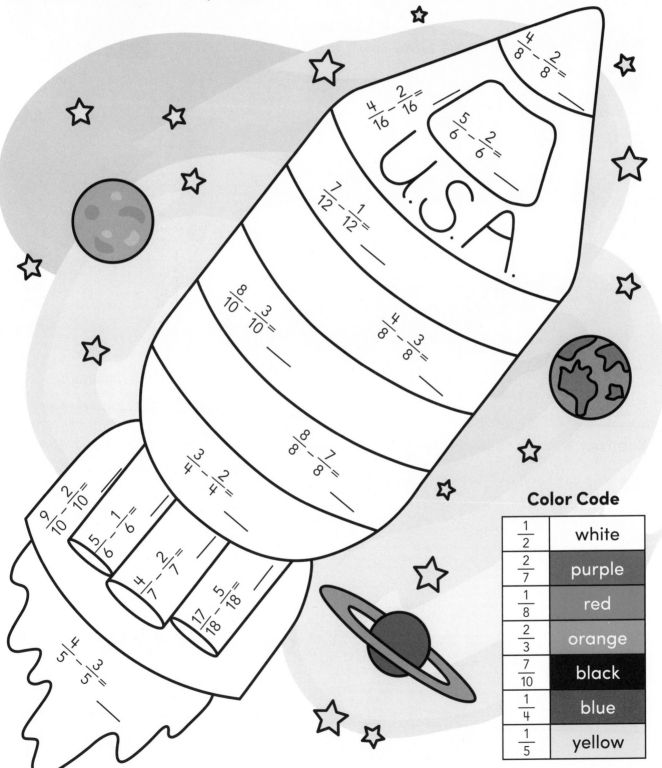

$$\frac{4}{8} - \frac{2}{8} =$$

$$\frac{4}{16} - \frac{2}{16} =$$

$$\frac{5}{6} - \frac{2}{6} =$$

$$\frac{7}{12} - \frac{1}{12} =$$

$$\frac{4}{8} - \frac{3}{8} =$$

$$\frac{8}{10} - \frac{3}{10} =$$

$$\frac{8}{8} - \frac{7}{8} =$$

$$\frac{3}{4} - \frac{2}{4} =$$

$$\frac{9}{10} - \frac{2}{10} =$$

$$\frac{5}{6} - \frac{1}{6} =$$

$$\frac{4}{7} - \frac{2}{7} =$$

$$\frac{17}{18} - \frac{5}{18} =$$

$$\frac{4}{5} - \frac{3}{5} =$$

Color Code

$\frac{1}{2}$	white
$\frac{2}{7}$	purple
$\frac{1}{8}$	red
$\frac{2}{3}$	orange
$\frac{7}{10}$	black
$\frac{1}{4}$	blue
$\frac{1}{5}$	yellow

What's the Difference

When subtracting fractions with like denominators,
subtract the numerators. The denominator does not change.

Subtract. Reduce to lowest terms.

1 $\dfrac{4}{10} - \dfrac{2}{10} =$

2 $\dfrac{7}{8} - \dfrac{3}{8} =$

3 $\dfrac{5}{6} - \dfrac{3}{6} =$

4 $\dfrac{2}{3} - \dfrac{2}{3} =$

5 $\dfrac{7}{4} - \dfrac{5}{4} =$

6 $\dfrac{6}{8} - \dfrac{1}{8} =$

When subtracting fractions with unlike denominators, find a common denominator
and make equivalent fractions.

Subtract. Reduce to lowest terms.

1 $\dfrac{1}{2} - \dfrac{1}{8} =$

2 $\dfrac{3}{5} - \dfrac{1}{10} =$

3 $\dfrac{3}{4} - \dfrac{1}{2} =$

4 $\dfrac{7}{10} - \dfrac{3}{5} =$

5 $\dfrac{1}{3} - \dfrac{1}{9} =$

6 $\dfrac{1}{3} - \dfrac{1}{12} =$

Ready to Reduce

The greatest common factor (GCF) of two numbers is the greatest number that is a factor of each. To reduce a fraction to lowest terms, follow these steps.

$$\frac{8}{12}$$

$$\frac{8 \div 4}{12 \div 4} = \frac{2}{3}$$

$$\frac{2}{3}$$

1. Find the greatest common factor.
Factors of 8 = 1, 2, 4, 8
Factors of 12 = 1, 2, 3, 4, 6, 12
The GCF = 4.

2. Divide the numerator and the denominator by the GCF.

3. Since 2 and 3 have no common factors other than 1, the fraction is in lowest terms.

Write the factors for the numerator and denominator.
Circle the greatest common factor.

1 Factors of 5: _____

Factors of 15: _____

2 Factors of 6: _____

Factors of 18: _____

3 Factors of 3: _____

Factors of 21: _____

4 Factors of 7: _____

Factors of 28: _____

Find the GCF. Reduce.

1 $\dfrac{4 \div}{10 \div}$ = ____

2 $\dfrac{4 \div}{20 \div}$ = ____

3 $\dfrac{7 \div}{21 \div}$ = ____

4 $\dfrac{6 \div}{12 \div}$ = ____

5 $\dfrac{3 \div}{21 \div}$ = ____

6 $\dfrac{3 \div}{24 \div}$ = ____

7 $\dfrac{3 \div}{12 \div}$ = ____

8 $\dfrac{5 \div}{15 \div}$ = ____

9 $\dfrac{7 \div}{28 \div}$ = ____

On each of 30 cards, write the numbers 1–30. Draw two cards. Find the greatest common factor for the two numbers. Continue until you have used all the cards.

Factor Flower

Find the greatest common factor (GCF) for each number. Then, color the picture.
Use the color key.

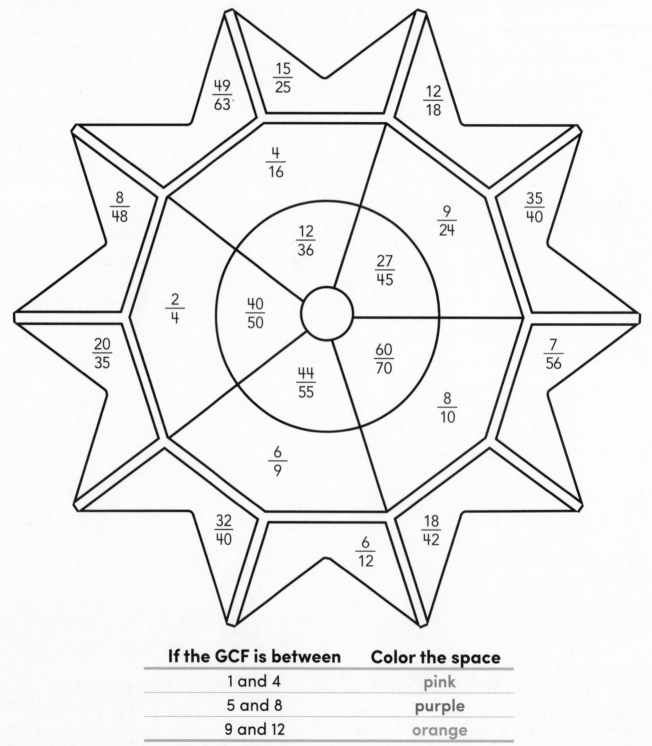

If the GCF is between	Color the space
1 and 4	pink
5 and 8	purple
9 and 12	orange

Fill in the other spaces with colors of your choice.

More, Less, or Equal?

Color the picture. Use the color key.

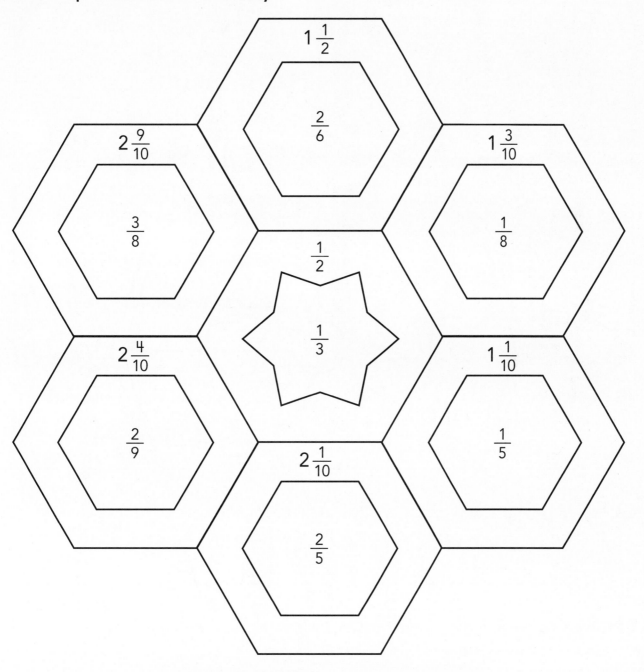

If the number is	Color the space
$> \frac{1}{2}$	blue
$= \frac{1}{2}$	purple
$< \frac{1}{2}$	green

White Socks, Black Socks

2 Rowena puts 7 socks in the washing machine. Four of them are black and 3 are white. What fraction of the socks is black? What fraction is white?

_____

3 Rowena hangs 8 socks out to dry. Two of the socks are black and 6 are white. What fraction is black? Write your answer in the simplest form.

_____

4 Judy Frog brings 6 socks on a trip. One third of the socks are red. The rest are green. How many socks are red? How many are green?

_____

 Judy has 12 socks. One third are white and one fourth are red. The rest are yellow. How many socks are yellow? How many socks are white and red?

Insect Inspection

Mrs. Smith's class took a field trip to the park. She explained how different insects grow to different lengths. This bar graph shows the insects in the park and how long each can grow. Use the graph to choose the best answer to each question below.

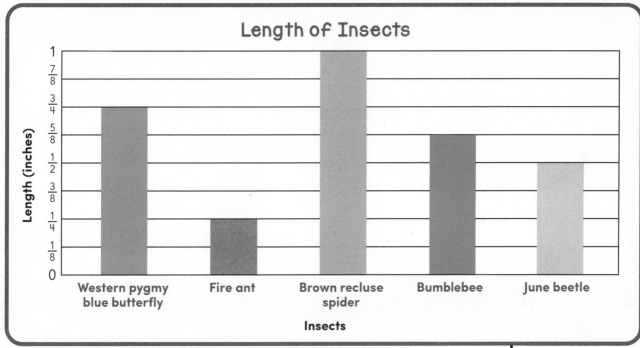

1. Which insect is the shortest?
   ○ fire ant   ○ bumblebee
   ○ june beetle   ○ western pygmy blue butterfly

2. How long is the butterfly?
   ○ $\frac{5}{8}$ in   ○ $\frac{3}{4}$ in
   ○ $\frac{1}{2}$ in   ○ 1 in

3. Which insect is twice as long as the june beetle?
   ○ bumblebee   ○ brown recluse spider
   ○ fire ant   ○ western pygmy blue butterfly

4. How much longer is the bumblebee than the fire ant?
   ○ $\frac{4}{8}$ in   ○ $\frac{1}{4}$ in
   ○ $\frac{3}{4}$ in   ○ $\frac{3}{8}$ in

Double Decimal Triangle

Color the picture. Use the color key below.

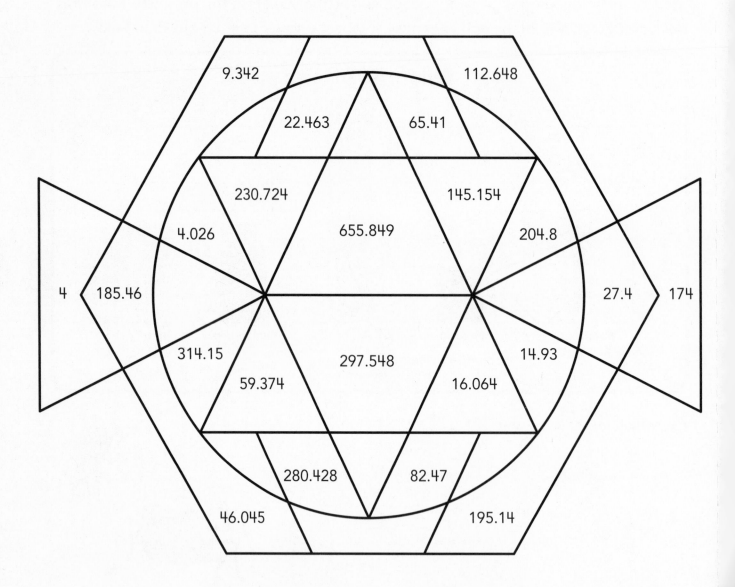

If the number has a	Color the space
4 in the ones place	green
4 in the tenths place	red
4 in the hundredths place	yellow
4 in the thousandths place	black

Fill in the other spaces with colors of your choice.

Exploding Star

Color the picture. Use the color key.

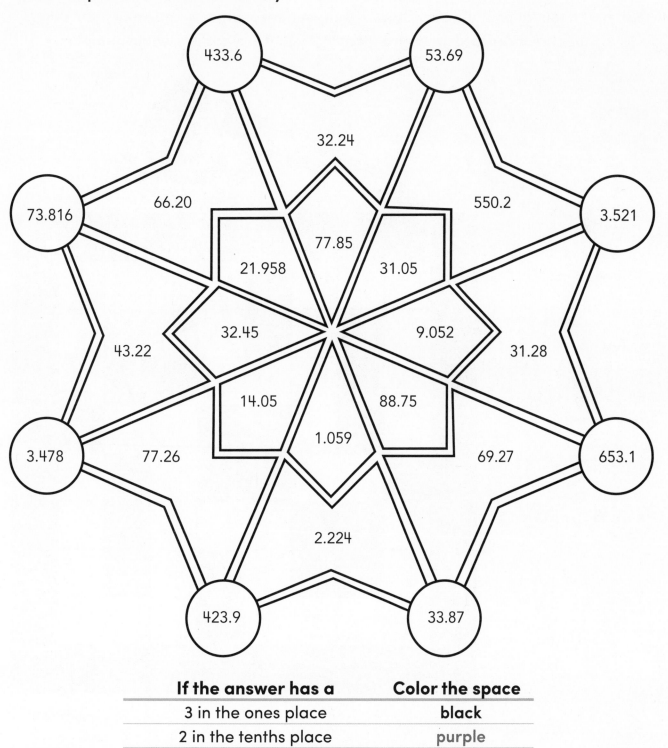

If the answer has a	Color the space
3 in the ones place	black
2 in the tenths place	purple
5 in the hundredths place	green

Fill in the other spaces with colors of your choice.

Across-and-Down Decimals

Add. Complete the cross-number puzzle as if it were a crossword puzzle. Give each digit and decimal point its own square. Remember to align the decimal points and add any necessary zeroes, then proceed as if you were adding whole numbers.

ACROSS

A. 1.3 + 2.4

C. 2.2 + 2.18

E. .3 + .25

F. .3 + .3

G. .56 + .34

J. .4 + .17

K. 6.93 + .23

L. 1.18 + 3.12

DOWN

A. 1.44 + 1.7

B. 23.11 + 53.18

C. 2.25 + 2.25

D. 6.5 + 1.6

F. .1604 + .11

H. 20.8 + 3.5

I. 1.367 + .333

J. .2 + .16

© Scholastic Inc.

Yard Sale

When you make change, always start with the price. Count on from the price. Start with the coins that have the least value. Calculate the change from these purchases.

① Lawn Game

Amount given: $5.00
Price: 3.45

Change: $ _____

⑥ Action Toy

Amount given: $10.00
Price: 6.49

Change: $ _____

② Yo-Yo

Amount given: $3.00
Price: 2.77

Change: $ _____

⑦ Sunglasses

Amount given: $4.00
Price: 3.68

Change: $ _____

③ Bike Helmet

Amount given: $10.00
Price: 7.55

Change: $ _____

⑧ Backpack

Amount given: $20.00
Price: 9.35

Change: $ _____

④ Soap Bubbles

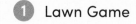

Amount given: $2.00
Price: 1.52

Change: $ _____

⑨ Jump Rope

Amount given: $4.00
Price: 3.17

Change: $ _____

⑤ Paint Set

Amount given: $20.00
Price: 7.30

Change: $ _____

⑩ Markers

Amount given: $5.00
Price: 2.43

Change: $ _____

Money Magic Puzzle

Round your answers to
the nearest dollar. Circle
the correct amount,
then fill in the puzzle.

ACROSS:

A. $16.98 + $18.99	$36	$26
C. $24.85 + $29.99	$65	$55
E. $21.99 + $8.95	$31	$41
G. $218.04 + $67.90	$286	$386
I. $53.75 + $40.98	$105	$95
K. $7.99 + $19.70	$28	$22
L. $99.98 + 99.57	$300	$200
M. $65.75 + $20.90	$87	$97
O. $9.69 + $32.99	$40	$43
P. $588.95 + $14.90	$704	$604
Q. $3.75 + $9.99	$13	$14
R. $428.70 + $50.90	$480	$520

DOWN:

B. $28.59 + $33.95	$69	$63
C. $39.25 + $18.70	$58	$42
D. $376.35 + $184.50	$521	$561
F. $7.28 + $11.69	$19	$16
H. $199.80 + $224.99	$525	$425
J. $399.95 + $126.99	$527	$566
M. $5.85 + $76.95	$83	$75
N. $39.80 + $13.99	$54	$62
O. $26.98 + $16.89	$44	$49
P. $48.95 + $18.99	$68	$66

Time for Play

The dogs in the neighborhood play in the park at the same time every day. Today, some are running around trees, and others are playing catch with their owners. But most of them are busy doing something else—chasing another dog! What time were they chasing the dog? Equivalent measurements can help you find the answer.

There are two answers next to each question. Circle the letter after the correct answer. When you've finished, write each circled letter in the blanks below the riddle. Be sure to write the letters in order.

1	How many weeks are in a year?	34	**L**	52	**T**
2	How many inches are in a foot?	12	**W**	36	**A**
3	How many centimeters are in a meter?	100	**E**	1,000	**O**
4	How many nickels are in a dollar?	40	**M**	20	**N**
5	How many days are in a year?	365	**T**	245	**S**
6	How many inches are in a yard?	36	**Y**	24	**B**
7	How many ounces are in a pound?	16	**A**	12	**I**
8	How many hours are in a day?	48	**C**	24	**F**
9	How many years are in a decade?	50	**H**	10	**T**
10	How many cups are in a pint?	2	**E**	4	**U**
11	How many quarts are in a gallon?	4	**R**	8	**D**
12	How many feet are in a mile?	5,280	**O**	2,160	**G**
13	How many seconds are in a minute?	30	**J**	60	**N**
14	How many millimeters are in a meter?	1,000	**E**	1,500	**P**

What time is it when 20 dogs run after 1 dog?

___ ___ ___ ___ ___   ___ ___ ___ ___   ___ ___ ___ ___ ___

Measure by Measure

Josie is surrounded by all kinds of measurement tools. She knows that a ruler measures the length of something. But she's not sure which of the other tools do what! Try giving Josie a hand.

Josie's Tool Box

Yardstick	Thermometer
Measuring tape	Clock
Measuring cup	Ruler
Scale	Teaspoon

Take a look at the list of measuring tools in Josie's tool box. Use the list to answer the questions below.

1 What tool could Josie use to measure the weight of a pumpkin? _____

2 What tool could Josie use to measure the width of her math book?

_____

3 Josie plans to watch one of her favorite televisions shows. What tool could help her measure the length of each commercial that appears during that show?

_____

4 Josie has an awful cough. What tool could she use to measure the amount of cough syrup she should take?

_____

5 If Josie's mom wants to find out Josie's temperature, which tool could she use?

_____

6 Say Josie wanted to make a cake. What tool could she use to measure the milk she needs?

_____

 Choose four of the measuring tools in Josie's Tool Box. Make a list of things you could measure with each of those tools.

Picnic Area

Area measures the number of square units inside a shape. Find the area of each ant family's picnic blanket by counting the number of squares on the blanket. Then, answer the following questions.

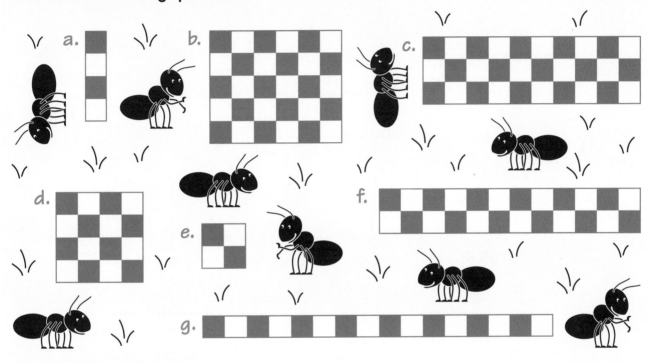

1. Which pairs of blankets have the same area?

_____ and _____

_____ and _____

_____ and _____

2. Which two blankets can you put together to make a rectangle with an area of 20?

_____

3. Which three blankets can you put together to make a rectangle with an area of 50?

_____

4. What is the total area of all of the ants' blankets?

_____

Perimeter and Area Zoo

To find the **perimeter**, count the sides of the units. To find the **area**, count the number of whole units.

A shape doesn't have to be a square or a rectangle to have perimeter and area. The animals in this zoo are different shapes. Can you find each animal's perimeter and area?

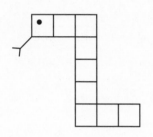

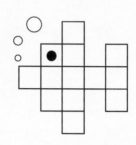

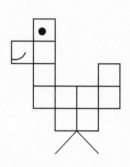

1 Perimeter _____

Area _____

2 Perimeter _____

Area _____

3 Perimeter _____

Area _____

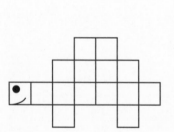

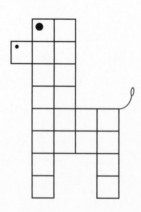

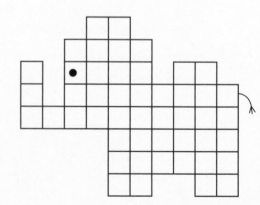

4 Perimeter _____

Area _____

5 Perimeter _____

Area _____

6 Perimeter _____

Area _____

Measuring and Classifying Angles

Right angle – looks like the corner of a square. It measures exactly 90°.

Obtuse angle – wider than a right angle. It measures greater than 90° but less than 180°.

Acute angle – narrower than a right angle. It measures greater than 0° but less than 90°.

Straight angle – two rays that make what looks like a straight line. It measures 180°.

Use a protractor to measure each angle. Then, decide whether it should be classified as acute, obtuse, or right.

 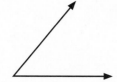

Angle measurement: _____

Angle classification: _____

Angle measurement: _____

Angle classification: _____

 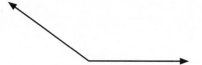

Angle measurement: _____

Angle classification: _____

 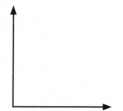

Angle measurement: _____

Angle classification: _____

Angle measurement: _____

Angle classification: _____

Flying Through the Air

Find the other half of each shape. To solve the riddle, find the question number at the bottom of the page. Then, use your answers and the Decoder to fill in the blanks.

① _____

② _____

③ _____

④ _____

⑤ _____

⑥ _____

⑦ _____

⑧ _____

⑨ _____

⑩ _____

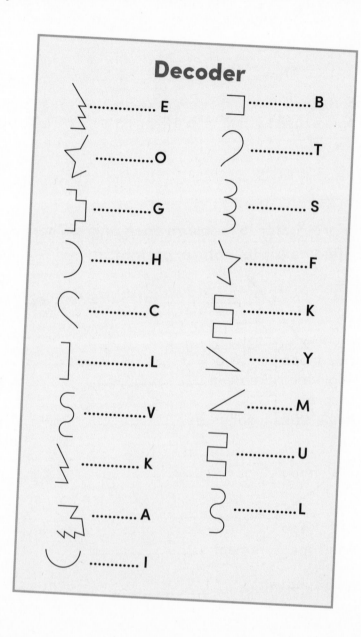

Decoder

.... E   .... B

.... O   .... T

.... G   .... S

.... H   .... F

.... C   .... K

.... L   .... Y

.... V   .... M

.... K   .... U

.... A   L

.... I

What is the last thing that the trapeze flier wants to be?

___ ___ ___   ___ ___ ___ ___   ___ ___ ___
 6   3   9   4   10 1   7   5   8   2

Shape Up!

How well do you know geometric shapes? Here's your chance to test yourself. Take a look at the shape in each statement. Fill in the blank spaces with the correct answers. When you're done, write the letters in the shaded squares on the spaces provided to solve the riddle.

1. An ⬡ has ____ ____ ____ ____ sides.

2. This triangle has an angle that is the opposite of obtuse.

   It's an ____ ____ ____ ____ angle.

3. The ____ ____ ____ ____ ____ ____ ____ of this rectangle is fourteen.

4. The ____ ____ of this rectangle is twelve.

5. This shape ☐ is a ____ ____ ____ ____ ____.

6. This shape ▱ is a ____ ____ ____.

7. This shape △ is a ____ ____ ____ ____ ____.

8. This shape ◯ is a ____ ____ ____ ____.

9. These shapes ⬡ ⬠ ⬡ have many sides:

____ ____ ____ ____ ____ ____ ____.

What did the alien eat for lunch?

____ ____   ____   ____ ____ ____.

Terrific Tessellations

What do math and art have in common? Everything—if you're making tessellations!

A **tessellation** (tess-uh-LAY-shun) is a design made of shapes that fit together like puzzle pieces. People use tessellations to decorate walls and floors, and even works of art.

This sidewalk is formed from rectangles.

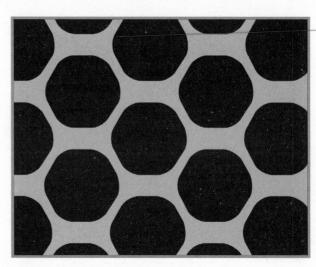

Hexagons form this beehive.

Here is a tessellation made from more than one shape.

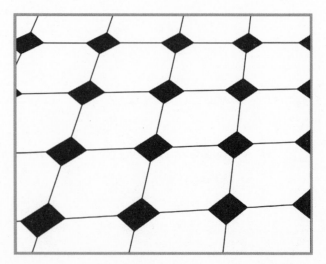

Squares and octagons form a tile floor.

Terrific Tessellations

Here's how you can make your own tessellation.

1 Start with a simple shape like a square. (Cut your shape from the heavy paper.) Cut a piece out of side A . . .

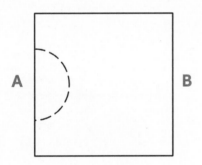

2 . . . and slide it over to side B. Make sure it lines up evenly with the cutout side, or your tessellation won't work. Tape it in place on side B.

3 If you like, do the same thing with sides C and D. Now you have a new shape.

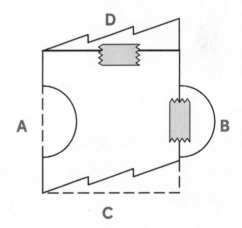

4 Trace your new shape on paper. Then, slide the shape so it fits together with the one you just traced. Trace it again. Keep on sliding and tracing until your page is filled. Decorate your tessellation.

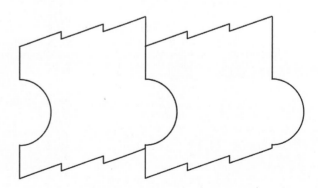

ANSWER KEY

Page 5
Answers will vary. Possible answers:
1. 496, 23 or 499, 26 **2.** 49, 63 or 43,
69 **3.** 23, 496 or 26, 493 or 93, 426 or
96, 423 **4.** 732, 469 **5.** 23, 64, 97 or
23, 67, 94 or 24, 63, 97 or 24, 67, 93
or 27, 63, 94 or 27, 64, 93 or 42, 63,
79 or 42, 69, 73 or 43, 62, 79 or 43,
69, 72 or 49, 63, 72 or 49, 62, 73
6. 674, 392

Page 6

Page 7
1. 10 **2.** 20 **3.** 50 **4.** 90 **5.** 200
6. 400 **7.** 600 **8.** 300 **9.** 500 **10.** 700
A "BUZZY" SIGNAL

Page 8
1. 41, +8 **2.** 100, +5 **3.** 77, +6
4. 85, +3 **5.** 68, –5 **6.** 68, –6
7. 74, +9 **8.** 70, +8 **9.** 55, –4
10. 86, +7 **11.** 56, +9 **12.** 47, –2
13. 55, +4 **14.** 47, –8 **15.** 54, –9
16. 83, +2 **17.** 33, –7 **18.** 77, +9
19. 50, –3 **20.** 67, +5

Page 9
1. T **2.** R **3.** R **4.** B **5.** O
6. O **7.** E **8.** O **9.** F **10.** E
LOTS OF ROOT BEER

Page 10
1. Deluxe Scraps **2.** Kibble or
Mouse Crumbs **3.** Mouse Crumbs
4. Table Scraps and Mouse Crumbs
5. Crumbs & Cheese and Deluxe
Scraps

Page 11
1. 1,804 **2.** 689 **3.** 1,063 **4.** 2,133
5. 3,489 **6.** 8,234 **7.** 7,538 **8.** 8,292
9. 5,429 **10.** 10,439
SPONGE CAKE

Page 12

Page 13
Across: 2. 1,807 **6.** 90,213 **8.** 35,975
9. 1,321 **10.** 17,496 **11.** 2,072
12. 686,552 **14.** 1,829 **15.** 6,317
Down: 1. 3,131 **3.** 6,956 **4.** 7,761
5. 45,044 **7.** 37,127 **10.** 12,697
13. 666,372

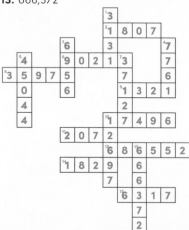

Page 14

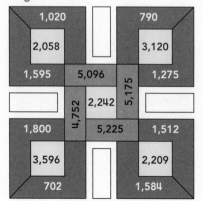

Page 15

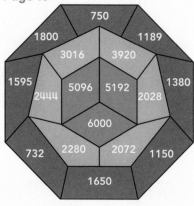

Page 16
D. 11 **E.** 20 **G.** 12 **A.** 4 **H.** 9 **N.** 18
I. 8 **O.** 7 **M.** 5 **Y.** 48 **R.** 6 **T.** 3
A DAIRY GODMOTHER

Page 17
1. 4 **2.** 2 **3.** 6 **4.** 5 **5.** 8 **6.** 4
7. 6 remainder 6 **8.** 9 remainder 2
9. 8 remainder 1 **10.** 15 remainder 2
"MULTI" PLIERS

Page 18

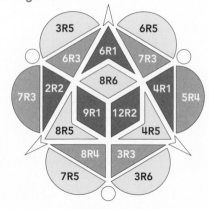

Page 19
1. 4 + 4 = 8mm long
2. 100,000 x 8 = 800,000 eggs
3. 40 ÷ 8 = 5 inches long

Page 20
What fraction of the candy is left?
2/3. Check student's work.

Page 21

THEY ALREADY

$\frac{1}{5}$ $\frac{3}{8}$ $\frac{4}{6}$ $\frac{6}{8}$ $\frac{1}{2}$ $\frac{2}{3}$ $\frac{2}{3}$ $\frac{4}{6}$ $\frac{1}{2}$ $\frac{1}{3}$ $\frac{6}{8}$

HAVE BILLS.

$\frac{3}{8}$ $\frac{1}{2}$ $\frac{5}{6}$ $\frac{4}{6}$ $\frac{5}{12}$ $\frac{3}{4}$ $\frac{2}{9}$ $\frac{2}{9}$ $\frac{3}{5}$

Page 22

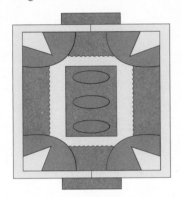

Page 23

1. 4/5 **2.** 1 **3.** 1 1/4 **4.** 5/7
5. 1 1/5 **6.** 2 **7.** 5/6 **8.** 1 3/7
9. 1 1/2 **10.** 2/3 **11.** 1 2/5 **12.** 4/9
13. 1 2/11 **14.** 1/2 **15.** 1 1/4

Page 24

A. 2/8 + 1/8 = 3/8 **D.** 3/9 + 1/9 = 4/9
S. 2/10 + 1/10 = 3/10 **I.** 2/16 + 1/16 =
3/16 **C.** 3/12 + 1/12 = 4/12 = 1/3
R. 4/8 + 1/8 = 5/8 **E.** 3/15 + 1/15 =
4/15 **T.** 5/10 + 1/10 = 6/10 = 3/5
E. 2/6 + 1/6 = 3/6 = 1/2 **I.** 4/16 + 1/16
= 5/16 **N.** 4/12 + 1/12 = 5/12
N. 6/12 + 1/12 = 7/12
SILENCE

Page 25

Page 26

1. 2/10 = 1/5 **2.** 4/8 = 1/2 **3.** 2/6 = 1/3
4. 0 **5.** 2/4 = 1/2 **6.** 5/8
1. 4/8 – 1/8 = 3/8
2. 6/10 – 1/10 = 5/10 = 1/2
3. 3/4 – 2/4 = 1/4
4. 7/10 – 6/10 = 1/10
5. 3/9 – 1/9 = 2/9
6. 4/12 – 1/12 = 3/12 = 1/4

Page 27

1. Factors of 5: 1, 5;
Factors of 15: 1, 3, 5, 15; GCF: 5
2. Factors of 6: 1, 2, 3, 6;
Factors of 18: 1, 2, 3, 6, 9, 18, GCF: 6;
3. Factors of 3: 1, 3;
Factors of 21: 1, 3, 7, 21, GCF: 3;
4. Factors of 7: 1, 7;
Factors of 28: 1, 2, 4, 7, 14, 28, GCF: 7
1. GCF: 2, 2/5 **2.** GCF: 4, 1/5
3. GCF: 7, 1/3 **4.** GCF: 6, 1/2
5. GCF: 3, 1/7 **6.** GCF: 3, 1/8
7. GCF: 3, 1/4 **8.** GCF: 5, 1/3
9. GCF: 7, 1/4

Page 28

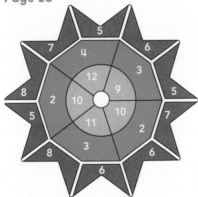

Page 29

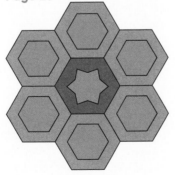

Page 30

1. 1/2 white, 1/2 black
2. 4/7 black, 3/7 white
3. 1/4 black
4. 2 red socks, 4 green socks
Extra Activity: 5 yellow socks,
7 white and red socks

Page 31

1. fire ant **2.** 3/4 in.
3. brown recluse spider **4.** 3/8 in.

Page 32

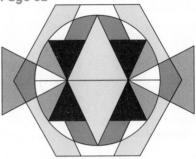

Page 33

Page 34

3	.	7		4	.	3	8
.		8		.			.
1		.	5	5			1
4		2			.	6	
	.	9			2		2
1		.	5	7			4
.			3		0		.
7	.	1	6		4	.	3

Page 35

1. $1.55 **2.** $0.23 **3.** $2.45 **4.** $0.48
5. $12.70 **6.** $3.51 **7.** $0.32 **8.** $10.65
9. $0.83 **10.** $2.57

Page 36

```
3 6 ■ ■ ■ 5 5
■ 3 1 ■ 2 8 6
4 ■ 9 5 ■ ■ 1
2 8 ■ 2 0 0 ■
5 ■ 8 7 ■ ■ 5
■ 4 3 ■ 6 0 4
1 4 ■ 4 8 0 ■
```

Page 37
1. 52 **2.** 12 **3.** 100 **4.** 20 **5.** 365
6. 36 **7.** 16 **8.** 24 **9.** 10 **10.** 2
11. 4 **12.** 5,280 **13.** 60 **14.** 1,000

TWENTY AFTER ONE

Page 38
1. scale **2.** ruler **3.** clock **4.** teaspoon
5. thermometer **6.** measuring cup

Page 39
1. a and e (4) b and c (30) d and g (16)
2. a and d **3.** a, b, and d **4.** 124

Page 40
1. perimeter: 20 area: 9
2. perimeter: 24 area: 13
3. perimeter: 22 area: 11
4. perimeter: 24 area: 15
5. perimeter: 32 area: 21
6. perimeter: 44 area: 48

Page 41
1. 50°, acute
2. 145°, obtuse
3. 170°, obtuse
4. 60°, acute
5. 90°, right

Page 42

1. **6.**

2. **7.**

3. **8.**

4. **9.**

5. **10.**

THE FALL GUY

Page 43
1. eight **2.** acute **3.** perimeter
4. area **5.** square **6.** cube
7. triangle **8.** circle **9.** polygons
IT ATE MARS BARS.

Page 44
Tessellate patterns will vary.